# *Because of a*
# *Great Longing*

# Robert N. Renard

Words Abound Press
Ventura   California

Because of a Great Longing

Copyright © 2016 by Robert Renard

Words Abound Press

ISBN: 978-0-6925-8306-7

Printed in the United States of America

# Contents

## Rear View Mirror                85

**The Ears Have It** *121*

**After Thoughts** **185**

# Foreward

Personally, I don't read poetry unless it is shoved in my face, sort of what Robert Renard did one night when he gifted me with a poem he composed shortly after a class I had taught. Out of respect I gave it a once-over. Then a twice. Then a thrice. Then, much to my surprise, asked him for more, and more he gave.

This is one poetry book I will enjoy reading from time to time, not only because the poems are clever but because they also brimming with inspiring wisdom, heartfelt joy, dramatic wonder and mind-tingling wit. While these poems reflect personal musings and insights lurking in the sharp mind of the author, they are sure to also kindle fresh awakenings of ideas and imagery in the reader. Skillfully worded and artfully sculpted, each phrase or prose, each thought and observation, makes its way quietly out of the page and onto the stage of the reader's mind where they provide quality entertainment, share uplifting life lessons, propose intriguing life questions, and awaken the spirit.

For those of us who enjoy poetry, this book is a welcome addition; for those of us who are not so much into poetry, this book will need to be brown-bagged, because we will want to carry it with us wherever we go without letting on that our reading habit has changed that dramatically.

Rabbi Gershon Winkler, PhD
Author of Magic of the Ordinary:
Recovering the Shamanic in Judaism

*To my loving wife*
*who has opened my eyes*
*to so much in my life.*

# *Clinks and Clashes*

## Abandoned

Guilt blocks his escape
self-destruction not an option
he must live
head in hands
abandoned
an orphan
a thin film of celluloid
his only protection.

## Turtled

Turtles carry their shells
as nature decrees
neck in mostly
sometimes out
stretching
just to get
somewhere
anywhere
hoping for a morsel of food
reward enough
for them
a real risk lived
perhaps I too
can learn.

## Awakened rudely by a Polish ex-priest going

Hey, it's six o'clock in the morning
a bit early for music,
the quiet of the campground
and my desired sleep disturbed.

He continues rocking to the beat of his music
from behind his shades,
no sorry expressed
only a thumbs up
like a motel clerk frankly unashamed
that my wake-up call was not requested.

He did not get a tip.

I left the next morning
early.

## Flower child

She rose gracefully
apparently invisible to the crowd
becoming a reflection of my past
memories flooding
1968
the summer of love.

I imagined her then
in the park
crowned with a flower garland
hair the color of ripe corn
bare-breasted
dancing her heart out
but not for us.

Now like then
she is pulled unashamed
to her feet in trail runners
a sun hat covers her graying curls
cargo shorts instead of a peasant dress
her blouse revealing bra straps
still dancing entranced
leaving us who could only sit
to watch.

## The best day of his life

It began as he approached up the hill
with wife at his side
his eyes locked on mine
seeking a place of protection
from the festival's blazing sun.

Like Joseph leading Mary
that long night of legend
seeking a safe roof
bedded with sweet clean hay
he asked me for shelter.

I as the innkeeper
made room for them
there in the lea of the tree.

This kindness he later proclaimed
became the beginning
of the best day of his life.

For me a mitzvah
easily given.

**Wishing to be touched**

Tail wagging
Up on tippy toes
All a bark
Hoping
To be touched
To play
Will soothe his yearning heart.

But dog must wait
Master's ear on a string
Cell leads his mind and body
Far away.

Too far to see the dog.

## Dragons

I am tired of writing.

emails
like old English sailing ships
never returning
so thought lost
over the end of the world
beyond
where the phrase *"here be dragons"* lies.

No more to give.

No battle in me for dragons.

## The Hillside

Fortnight lilies fan the hill
backed by purple-topped wands
crowning bushels of green swords
under the watchful gaze of ripening tangerines
heavy on their branches.

## Wanting

Wanting
for one
heralds
a challenge to overcome
a mountain to climb
glory
while for another
a source of suffering
how a spirit is broken
crushed down
still
the Light
flickers in the darkness
beckoning us on.

**Visions**

My monitor opens a window of visions
from yesterdays near forgotten
to the tomorrows
I cannot dream.

I hear our children laughing
a chorus only they can sing;
while seeing my son and his friends
topped with hats sharing
a cheesy smile from the *land down under*
where I will never tread.

And off with a click my heart
filled with my honey
and I buzzing round the grass
staking our claim
a weekend campsite
overlooking rock strewn beach
with crash of surf
and the passing whale
under the brightest of blue sky.

But best of all my fingers
dancing over the keys
transport me
to when I am alone with my bride
be it lands end
beneath the peaks
my favorite place
the taste of her kiss
flavors my lips.

## Clinks and Clashes

The lights
dimly lit
hanging in loops
from above
and beyond
the lights created by Him
twinkle.

We sit in rattan-cushioned chairs
filled with Oneg and
even sweeter the words
of Torah settle
in our hearts and minds.

The temple courtyard resounds
with our laughter
our questions of each other's lives
a hope about the week to come
freely our worries, dreams and challenges
dance between us under the lights.

So life is lived
with it's clinks and clashes
ups and downs
like a dish shared
with good friends
beneath the canopy of heavenly Light.

**I fell**

I fell into a hole in your life.

At the time it looked like the entrance to a
wonderful world
I venture forth into this new world
becoming a *piece* in your life
a passenger
not an adventurer
the illusion broke
reaching out
grabbed my life line
pulled free
beginning mine
and allowing you yours.

## Hula Hoop

She must have known we were watching
her unabashed gyrations
the hoop encircling her
caressing her
from the tip of her elbow
down each curve to her knees
and then up again
defying gravity and our gazes.

She must have known we were watching
as she softly met the hoop
not with a child's hula
but a caress
converting its energy
into her dance.

She entwined in the notes
swaying to the rhythm of the blues
bright sunshine surrounding
pines fragrant
intoxicating.

She must have known we were watching.

## Leaves

Like lemon teardrops
falling
through the shimmering rays
the morning sunrise
aglow
nurturing my heart.

## Swaying

With yellow and pink tops
green and purple centers
they look an odd pair
each so different
bodies soon encircle
arms entwine
hips touch
swaying in the music
enlivening their love.

## Perhaps

Empathy being the path
the way to overcome
becoming sensitive to others
heals my fear
lonely.

Today
apologizing for bumping it
a silent doorframe
reminded me
that taking my healing a bit too serious
creates loneliness, too.

## She Stood

His hair so gray
I noticed first
She stood near
Not touching
Separate
Something intruding
On what could be.

Both like the tall pines
Surrounding us
A ways apart so spreading limb and root
Would not interfere
Instead trees sharing
Life and sun
Water and earth
Swaying in the swirling music.

The couple
Still
Motionless
Then melting wordlessly
Into his shoulder
Her head nuzzled
Breathing in his scent
Arms entwined
A couple bursting
Blossoming
Becoming One.

And still she stood.

**Learn my heart**

I look up to see signs of healing
My wall collects
The thoughts
The words
The pictures
What is dear to me
A life well lived
Or just an advertisement
Of who I want to be.

I can only learn my heart
By noticing what comes from it
So I watch
The details of my life
Hoping to see me
A reflection
On my wall.

So I move
Living each day
Watching
Living
Hoping
That my actions
Will reflect well my heart.

Is it enough
I wonder.

## Kite
## Dreams

She spoke of her wishing
wishing for a freedom free of troubles.
She shared dreaming of a kite tethered thinly by
a thread connecting her present image to her hope
for a future. I cheered the delicate weave of that kite
string how strong it pulled nearly invisible to the
naked eye but oh so powerful in its work to
maintain the connection to pull her through
to her vision  one of  brighter tomorrows.
So it turns out her suffering now
did not stand a chance
against her life
the Light that
guides the
Weaver's
dream
of
her
life.

## A wind blows through the trees

A wind blows through the trees
we walk listening
the whirl
the whoosh
talk and listen
kind thoughts
reassure me.

Guessing
you dream
offering
I question.
then we both offer
reach for each other
fearlessly.

Bang the balls fly
caught in a torrent of blue sky
hit, hit, bunker, pitch
rake the grains
smooth
now the putt.

Are we in the fairway?
on the path?
answer
play on

piercing the pain
wrapped too long
around his heart
held silently
beyond reach
until risking
we trust
two men
on the green
in the wind.

Later now
you ask
is it time
play on
my reply
wrestling our pain to the surface
and for a moment
it is enough
we become
a bit freer in the world.

From high in the wind
you yell to me
Wow, what a great shot!
I listen hear you
still
helping me to notice the good
be patient
enjoy each day.

# *Who Created These*

## The Shining Times

When in those high mountain expanses
under the white depths of deep sleep
lives a yearning,
A promise...
an unknown which keeps.

The mountain men called it the Shining Times
the promised scent of bloom and earth
the sight of fresh hoof and feather
is borne anew out of the yearning of life...
A promise...
an unknown kept.

You are my shining meadow, my love, my life
enlivened out of unknown hopes held,
a new  wilderness of sights and breath which
have come to me
      An unknown...
a promise kept and keeping bright
      A Shining.

## I guess

In the quiet
I guess about what life is.

Learning comfort from
The good and the bad
Wisdom from
The glorious
Mixed with awful
Even in the so-so, unchangeable
I have found the stupendous.

It all surrounds
Enfolds.

Combining is the spice of it
Yours,
With Mine
Makes it rise.

**Fire**

Sirens screaming
flashing red lights
trucks and fighters surrounding
the power of transformation blazes skyward.

It draws forth smoke and cinders from
compressed trailer wall and garage roof
so strong solid against the wind and rain
now consumed melting
vanishing into the sky
a dark choking cloud of its elements.

We use the secret
water
it unlocks the mystery
consuming
soaked, charred, full of holes
what humans built of Earth
still stands.

We use the key
the water
unlocking the fire's grasp
not realizing it is a miracle
once again
creation
revealed.

## Burned

As i lay in bed
a small voice from within
sweet and powerful
a Spark
only a word or two
burned me
i knew at once
i could do it.

**Hide 'n go seek**

Invisible lines of connection
made of Light from the void
*ein sof*
the no thing place of becoming
where it all comes flowing out
most to disappear into hiding.

The Light waits,
desiring to be found
and lifted up
as I play hide 'n seek with Him
laughing out loud
at each new sighting.

## Finding Peace on the path

Legs in the air
arms reaching in vain
too late
the consequences of his folly
struck him

The jester
once clothed in sarcasm
now incased in bark
punished for his witty remarks
humor lost
on an unforgiving witch.

She cast her spell
revenge for his joking chiding
and he diving for cover
the boulder no protection
he is a tree
a hamadryad.

Down he went
into the earth
hands becoming roots
securely held
holding
his body a trunk
supporting the ever growing branches
that sprang from his outstretched legs
now pushing skyward.

A foliage of green
the stems
the leaves
crown him
the tree
he has become.

His prison now a blessing
longer trapped
trying to be human
worthy and good
he flourishes
blossoming freely
no regret
his shade nurtures me
this tree along the path
in the forest
content
at peace.

**Joy**

Bird in treetop
high above
hidden in plain sight.

Some see
others don't
I hope to.

## Lessons from the snake

Adam afraid
moved beyond truth
saying
don't touch.

The snake heard
showing Eve
the touching
she now doubting
Adam
failed the task.

To bring balance
like the snake
one must call
truth
into the Light
and see what comes.

## A Merry Tune

A merry tune
lingers
a memory
I strain to hear the pipe
my ears
my heart
left yearning.

## Wilderness

Hearing a cricket in Manhattan
as much an act of holiness
as hearing that small still voice within
drawing me nearer to You
in the hustle and bustle
of my life.

## Contrast

One shaker black
The other white
Words on the page
The paper white
The night black as pitch
Morning all aglow

Simple
My heart wishes.

**Drops of Nothingness in the bucket of everything**

Picturing myself
a borderless print
disappearing
to be elsewhere
my task
making more life
when others see less.

So elsewhere
becoming borderless
never even developed
knowing
it's a waste of time
since I am
already
looking.

## Guided

by words written
my mind
follows the trail
crumbs of reassurance
seasoned with faith
a place
refuge.

## Going out

going into the wilderness
is
playing outside the lines.

**Here**

The man looked through his pain
from outside the world
peering in
through the picture frame
that imprisoned him there
behind the clear glass
on my wall.

He isn't here
I said out loud
sadly
my thought escaping my lips.

The rabbi understood
laying a comforting arm
upon my waning shoulder
she whispered
you are not outside
you are here
with us.

## The door opening

I sit listening
bagels and cream cheese in hand
smiling mouths
sharing questions
comforted by my friends
and our Rabbi.

In this place
all is calm
predictable
when just behind her
the door opens
then closes a bit
creaking
the wind I think
then I notice
it is Him.

I wanted to tell them
to say look
there
it's Him…
but I was afraid
silent.

## Burned away

The wind blew fiercely that day
something ignited
there was a fire.

Today the two that burned
sway bravely in the wind
both appear healthy.

Inside the blackened truck
one tree rebounded
its foliage is green
round and full the palm's head
bounces in the breeze
reaching for the sun.

The other tree hurt
I notice through my window
daily its crown of green has faded
it is out of balance
the fire now long extinguished
burned away its spark of life.

It is doing well to survive
wanting to thrive again once more
held there in the ground
secured by roots
it must be a tree
it can do nothing more
than to stand its ground.

I, too, have been burned
not being a tree I can choose
stand or leave this place
endangered I move
nurturing my injured heart
hoping to improve my moment
and hopefully some that will follow.

## Between the two

The Zohar teaches
two forces work
together
the Light
and the evil inclination
each pushing
my most precious gift
free will
so my only path
lies between the two.

## All the way through

I gave her my map
my security blanket
the Siddur
found resting on the chair
foolishly believing
I could find my way.

The chants began
we all moved
and yes I did know the way
all the way home
Shabbat Shalom.

**Butterfly**

Watching a butterfly intuitively flit
blossom to blossom
in a clear sky of opportunity
above the garden
I wade through a swamp of indecision
heavy steps weighted down
by water and earth
bound by free will.

Choice a gift
instinct a blessing
seems to depend on my travel arrangements
most days.

**Wisdom**

When the importance of knowing
what things mean
gives way to
understanding
that things are more
than they really seem.

## Ayin

Between evening and day
On Shabbat
I find some
In the space.

She calls
An emergency
I can see it
She can not
She's scared.

I say look
See
There, right there
And yet fail to notice.

The leaves fall
Allowing the deep
Of sleep to cover me
While all along
The Eyes of God
Lovingly watch.

## Frame

Is the painting upside down
in the frame
the framer procrastinates
mounting what has been created
for fear of being discovered
wrong.

**First time**

Exiting the escalator steps
I saw her sitting there
waiting.
It was as though it were my first time.

Would she know?
Could she tell
I was not raised this way?

She laid down her phone
looked up and asked
*your name?*
Which one?
I thought
then decided and spoke.

She extended her hand looking at mine
And handing me my name badge
encased a plastic neck hanger.

Putting it on
collecting my folder
I was complete
I was in
a member
part of the tribe
I was a Jew
and I was ready!

## Make

this "no thing" place of non-being
the *ein sof*
inviting and ready
calling the *Shechinah*
to come with all her mysteries
and make.

**Rabbi**

Older teachers
I am used to
outside and foreign
from my childhood
no vowels
right to left they see
this one sweet and tender
of my family both
accustomed to
and new.

He is my son.
I know him
and yet now a teacher
to me and my fellows surprised
with respect
I approach him
to learn to know
him
in this new way.

A new trick for this old dog.

## Handiwork

So all my relations
earth, fire, wind and water
all are One.

Consumption is transmuting
the stardust and the Light
contained
the handiwork of the One
hidden.

Nothing is destroyed
all is broken
transformed.

## Soaring

I am a chant
a melody
of my mother's heart
dreaming me to soar.

Once grounded
empathy I seek
like baby's hair
against my cheek
a delicate cascade
to soothe my heart.

But finding little
brings on worry
exploring within
I forget my song.

Struggling
my soul lifts once more
soaring
becoming song
with chorus and verse
my life rings out
a blessing.

## Why

From outside to in
the what, how and why
seek to make a sale.

Inside out
the why becomes the source
the starting point
creating a connection
between all who want
to do a what
so a how
will benefit the whole.

Tikkun Olam.

## The Sages Dance

The ancient words jump and sway on the surface
enlivened by the beating
the sapling's branch wrapped in deerskin brings
its blows striking the drum
announce the sage's wisdom
is soon to flow.

I sit watching the symbols dance.

Rabbi's heart a blaze
the drum resounds each beat
the Hebrew dances on the hide
and in my mind
leaving footprints of
Light, truth, justice and love
in its path
as it winds through me.

I am an open book
in need rewriting
by this dance
listening
a song of prayer and power
bathes me in wisdom
soothing my pain
allowing me to see
life.

Watching the ancient symbols
dancing there on the deerskin
I feel
its pounding
guiding my heart
into the magic.

## Tzimtzum *the first withdrawal*

If God initiated existence
by extending Himself
there would be
no me
no place for creation
no thing
all places would be filled with Him.

To create
He hollowed out a place
withdrawing
a void made ready
a rainbow filled with His loving light
bright in places
showing itself a gift
freely given.

Other parts hidden
waiting for us
hoping we will seek
glimpses offered
hinting at the way
inviting us to be emblazoned
like Moses at the bush.

The rainbow's promise
conceals the Shechinah's mystery
the refracting Light
reveals an invisible glow
only to our inner sight.

## Faith

Reveal yourself
or see nothing
and never be seen.

Bare
uncovered
like that day
in the garden.

Today
show your self
to be seen
by the One
unseeable.

## For now

The sages teach
we only live
long enough to accomplish
our life's work.

For now
I will continue
to add my voice to the choir.

## Midbar

In the wilderness
at my essence
desire must emerge
igniting passion
inviting the meeting
so that love will join
me.

**Staring**

It stares back at me
blank
the computer screen
black fire on white fire
seeking to become something
more.

Like staring down a well
the glass is dense
darker than I can bear
a reflection.

Then
suddenly
out they come
a stream of words
from this cavern inside
thought empty.

Rich precious images
minded by my fingers
tapping the keys
forming
what my heart yearns to say.

## Becoming wilderness

One that is unsuspecting
is paired with another
unwilling
brought together
from the far side of the world.

This is me coming to my beloved.

A child of the fifties
working class
to cowboy student
Methodist
questioning too much
separating self from the fold
not knowing
the path
it was leading
to my tribe.

Seeking my home of comfort
finding wilderness
where I alone
unprotected by my illusions
free to be who I am
or free to pretend
to be someone else
facing
being only who I can be

present
afraid
and looking.

Thinking my home a carriage
traveling in comfort
on a road
now able to go out
to "follow after wisdom and holiness"
my house becomes an empty place
filled with plenty
which has always been there
but for the carriage
I was never supposed to be a ride.

So being out
I walk behind
the path
suddenly appears
like Jacob
finding
he was
in this place and I…
I did not know it
so finding
my beloved
and Him
on bethel.

• from a story about  Reb. Elimelech of Lizensk

**The tribe**

Elders stuck
Down
Now in death barricades
Against the cold and the wind
Protecting the young ones
All this to rebuild the tribe
Here to hold the hillside.

Then brush and wildflower
Oak and grass
Came blown in on the wind
Welcome guests at first
Helping hold the earth
Fast against the spring run off
But their nature to flower and seed
To make where forest has been
Their new shady home.

To this new challenge the tribe arises
From elder tree to sapling pine to delicate sprout
The word is passed on
Renewal
Faith
Future and Life
Hineni
we are here.

The tribe makes its stand.

## Covenant

Steamy, heavy breath precedes me
up the mountain
as I seek more.

Following the cloud that
flows from my lips
the breath of life
a shared gift
guiding me
drawing me closer
to You.

# *Rear View Mirror*

## Rear view mirror

We raced to save our lives
that cold dark night
fearing being beaten to death.

Away from the car too small
for the refrigerator-sized older boyfriends
streaming out like killer clowns
under the big top
straight from hell
going to kill us
all for a few words
sweet talk and smiles
to the girls we found wandering there.

Terrified we peeled
out
perfect timing
my partners later said
lost them in the stadium
lot too fast
too scared
laughing
looking in my rear view mirror
and for weeks to follow.

I was the hero then.

## Safety

Rolling
laughing
down the hill
the game turned
terrible
without warning.

The waterfall below
closing on its prey
devouring
first my screams
and next me.

I saw it all
the flash
down I went
drowning in the ocean
cold
alone
without a chance.

At the brink
he came lifting me
and up
into his big strong arms
I went.

Safe
my world put right
in my daddy's arms.

## My Shield

I sit watching
an image of myself
from before.
A picture on the wall
me sitting
watching my dad fishing
before he left.

Sandwich in hand
my feet propped up on a log
under the bluest of skies
kissed by waves
lapping at the shore and me
safe behind the log.

He was barrel-chested
larger than life
his pole in hand
plumbing the depths
and the miracles he brought me
on his hook
oh what a delight.

This memory is sweet
without those days
warm in the sunlight me
a kid savoring the peanut butter & jelly
relaxed and safe
I would be defenseless
now.

Remembering
being protected
watched
and loved by my dad
becomes my shield today.

## Pebble Beach Escape

Nine years old
trapped in the car
with my relatives
when from the backseat
I spied it.

White on green amidst the wood
it shone bright as the lighthouse torch
to my dreaded fog
there in the doldrum
of the black Studebaker from hell.

Stop my voice boomed
so loud my mother screeched
brakes applied
the door flung open
to freedom I escaped
my torture ended
off on an adventure
to capture my prize
an abandoned golf ball
my reward
for the hours of being a good boy
so quiet
in my cell.

My gift in hand,
a Titlist golf ball
number 1
in my grasp
squeezed with pleasure.

I now beckoned back
Come, let's go
and I returned
to my captivity.

Today at fifty nine
my eyes glued to the US Open golf match
at Pebble Beach once more
this time spirit free searches
the course
to spy that spot again
and relive that moment
in happiness and freedom.

## Scout Master

His garage like the wood shop at school
smelling mostly of pine
except the jars on the shelves
were filled with fire crackers
not screws.

## Dave Goldman's Seder

On the way to see the Doors
that night
I found myself Elijah
at a door
made open.

Bidding me welcome
the voices called
from deep within
come in.

Entering
the laughter of parents
the scowls of elders in ties and suits
distracted
I missed His invitation
but not the path.

## He was

He was good at it
the grades
the girls
sports
and cheeseburgers with fries.

I looked up to him
music played at lunch
piano and sax in the band room
audience at the door.

His best friend
the driver of the car
at late night rallies
second to his first presidency
then he to mine
equipment guy to his band
an almost member.

His buddy
money in my hand
always ready to have fun
Fillmore West
magical milk bus odyssey
cribbage when grounded
dances when not.

We went till times they did change.

The last time we met
he looked just like his father
and I suppose
I did too.

## My mom

She chose to be alone
knowing there was
safety in the power of one.

Not the One
she had long ago
abandoned Him
too many losses
her father
an eldest brother
and her mother's affection
withdrawn after she married my father.

All took their toll
her change exhausted
by the time I
a youngster first saw
the sadness my father
inflicted.

The night shift her shield
against loving
one that could hurt her
we kids the second line of defense
she always put us first
so no time
no energy for a relationship.

She played it safe
as they used to say
what chance would she have
a divorcée with kids
and older too.

Then she returned
to Solvay
her 50th reunion found him there
widowed
lonely
and Ed his name
remembered
still held a spark in his heart
just for her.

## Getting better

Head down
sideways laying
on my arm
a comforting pillow
there in the pews
tears and sobs releasing
coming from somewhere
deep inside my past.

My father gone
to the state hospital
not for surgery
not for medicine
to return him well
instead the electroshock therapy
charging his anger at my mother
suffering
dulling the glint once held in his eyes
just for me
I thought
don't think about it
don't feel
it will get better.

Too late
I became
the little man of the family
my childhood cut short
the toy bringer now scary
unrelenting
bible quoting
not my father any more.

This week in temple
my tears flowing
I turn over my memories and
the question echoes- will it get better
He whispers the promise softly
inside me
yes.

## Clarinet Twins in German class

The clarinet twins from band
in my German class
what luck!

In awe
I was speechless
not a note did I produce

## 1910

An engraved plaque names her
at the archway white skin covers
bright pastel hues of yellows and greens
inside
a walk now of slow
fearful steps
once a rush of horses' hooves
carriage wheels
and ambulance tires screeching.

She born out of an earthquake
new and sturdy
a safe place for hoped repair of body
they were driven
now of broken mind and spirit they
come
her warm aching halls they wander
searching and being found
yearning to walk
in the small tree lined lawn
still her wide pride
welcoming
those in need of
repair and rest.

## Natural

They said I was a natural
my first thought
at what?

## How the deputy got Sunder loaded

Four hooves at the ready
one-eyed tail snorting
the Deputy chewing cigar
puffing
left hand on the rope
right wrapped round horse ear
an eye to eye stare down.

The trailer at once prize and prison
pawing the air no more
carried in by his ear
the ramp up
Old Smoky the victor
Sunder was loaded.

**Dick always used protection with his girlfriends**

the gate a moat
a dog the bell
Dick already up.

## A flutter in the night

A flutter in the night
but not my heart
a lost butterfly
ripped open my dreams.

## Sammy the Cat catches a big one

Up on the hill they call
dogs racing all barks
jaws salivating
in the heat.

Sammy
double lids closed
the shade nurturing her cool
dreams tasting squirrel
later.

Dogs fooled
ripping earth
squirrels all a chuckle
their plan a success
dogs made wide
their den's entrance
dirt cleared again.

That night
Sammy the Dagger
a squirrel's heart did she pierce
a gift left
served warm
at cool of dawn
on my door mate
one big squirrel
to share with me
and nearby
Sammy all a glow.

## Hal thought less

none under his hat
bitter taste in my mouth
mud tipped boots tells all.

## Mr. Farris's nail

molten ferrous pounded
square removed fossil
extract of an old porch.

## Jim Lopper didn't lope anymore

Boiling down hot uphill trail
his limp gave way to a fall
the bed of a pickup
his flying carpet home.

## Dillon

horse hunkering
rain drenched muddy
up on the hill ears down.

## The Secret Lagoon

She and I
our dog made three
the boat banged
by oars
tickled by Sky's dog nails
giggles and laughter erupting
blue sky
water wet
combining
a merry calliope.

Gliding
cross Lake Maimie
dodging mountain peaks
reflected
passing over tree tops
high
racing clouds floating
swift
time stood still
that special day
loved and loving.

And all along
we three
a sail on Puff's gigantic tail.

## Zippered

Breathe of the years
separating us
escapes as the zipper
follows its path
one tooth to the next.

The imagined scent
of joys and family accomplishments
perfumes my memory
first tickets to Disneyland
honors for this and that
the *Daddy I love you* cards
funny pictures
invitations to school musicals
and your hand-made birthday cards
I thought would never end
and there
at the end
the *I hate you* letter
you wrote me at thirteen
for not letting you grow up.

The pages stop turning
shut well
you're all grown up now
and gone
no birthday cards for me.

Scrapbook embossed on the cover
screams
as I zipper
it safely
back in to time
and it's protective
see-through bag
sadly accepting
it is just too much for me
today.

## The warning

The mommy snake
and its baby
slithering toward me
black-eyed
along the bottom of the pool
smooth
gliding
effortlessly.

I tried to swim
panic stricken
but too afraid to look away
I ran
backwards as it was
flailing
desperate to escape them
their teeth
bearing down on me.

Chest-deep water
held me motionless
in its clutches
snared like animal
paw in a steel trap.

Screaming for help
the man calmly smoking at poolside
his cigarette in a gnarled hand

did nothing
said nothing.

Exhausted
splashing
breathless
slipping under the surface
the end was near
their teeth
razor sharp
struck.

I awoke
and the real nightmare began.

# *The Ears Have It*

## Weird

Healing worthlessness
feels discouragingly sad
disappointing
as it becomes
a genuinely wonderful
expression of self-worth
weirdly true.

## Welcoming

Desiring to welcome
I consider inviting
others
facing my fears.

Once they come
can I
be present
take down the
pain
the three inches of bullet-proof glass
encasing me.

Turtles
must
to get anywhere.

## Undergone

Believing
choosing to go
seeing all that was spread before me
after a great longing
I am challenged anew
excited
looking.

Later the surface parted
revealing the blessing
I had undergone.

**Too**

Did you survive
the party
a funny question
too serious
for honesty.

## Loneliness

Lack of sunlight strikes my stem
On the rich forest floor
Nearby trunks lift the canopy high
Envy ensues as I
Long to be what I am not

Wishing to join them
Neath the source of life
Emptiness fills me
Surrounded in the shadows
I am left
Silently wishing.

## The ears have it

Leaving my door
chirping entered
umbrella lifted
the ears have it
sounds pour in
refreshing
beating my drum.

## It's sign

Is it *it's* or it is it *its,*
she asked.
i don't know, i replied,
showing my ignorance.

Coincidence?
a sign?

Embarrassed I laughed
believing
I had guessed wrong
made an error
been lacking
again.

Later, it turned out
she wrote *it's* too!
But I knew
it was a blessing
a message
sent small
to show me
my ego.

**Away**

Lonely hurt one
to a new place hope flies
triple threats like leaves fall.

## A Merry Tune

A merry tune
It lingers
A memory
I strain to hear the pipe
My ears
My heart
Left yearning.

## Rocking Chair

Straight-backed
still
calm
sitting
and listening.

It did not rock.

It did not want.

It was content.

**Fear**

is being alone in a crowed room

thought happy when sad inside

seen but not heard, so misunderstood
watching keen eyed
everyone

finding knowing so much
does not help

wanting but holding back

missing and being missed
too late to matter

the dark

the quiet

the loving touch
too terrifying to receive.

**Family trees**

Framed by my window
four trees bend and blend in the wind
roots intertwined
nurtured in earth shared
seem happy together
swaying in the breeze.

Like four branching limbs
the family
shares a table
entwining nurturing.

I outside
sadly wish
to be rooted there.

**Me**

I have a new relationship with my son
and I don't know why.

I have an old relationship with my daughter
and I don't know what it is.

Sadly, these relations seem mostly lost
on me
but only mostly.

## Crying

Tears come sometimes too easily
touched my leaking begins
others watch worrying
scared that this water
falling from my eyes
is something bad.

I worry too
but don't ask.

## Too Late

She was young and
seeking
until she donned her grandmother's clothes
then she was finished
too soon
too young.

## Trees bow lightly in the presence of squirrels

white birch saplings sway
pine trunks motionless in shade
squirrel paws bounce between
all the way home.

**It happened as easy as**

**One**
She is mad
at me
for being myself
easily surprised.

**Two**
Desperate
animal trapped
not understood
groping for a way out
errant words exchanged
rejection felt.

**Three**
Hurt
unsure
not good enough
together seeking.

## Fireman sparking

*Are you pouring yet?*
I ask
the fireman clad brewer replied *yes*
*You have what I want,*
I said.
*Only beer,*
sending me a twinkling-eyed smile
flirting he continued
*I have a husband.*

Laughing, I accepted his playful complement.

## Peter

Rock me
but not my boat.

## Out of nowhere

Reading in growing darkness
watched by trees
their knotty eyes on me
seeming to know the words
I stop.

Their gaze strips me
my cool aloof
uncovered
a fear
I don't much like showing
my eyes closed by shame.

How good are you

Out of no where
echoes from my past
thunder
I can not avoid
laid open
suffering.

My darting eyes
desperate
when one of the trees
looks back
his face cracked and worn
like a father
he beckons me to come near
wordlessly his old eyes are full
damp and warm
compassion offered
so freely
I drink.

## Degrees

hot windless baking
on an endless day
waves breaking on sand
too far away.

## Thrilling

Unknown before
now well and deeply felt
your bouquet surrounds me
our lives entwined
like a bear entering a meadow in spring
drawn by your sweet scent.

**Still in your presence**

In the quiet
is the wonder
the bliss
the giggle
and the butterfly's wing.

In the quiet
appears a painted sky
at dawn
by God's stroke
there
and the gentle touch of you
hand in hand
drawn
to watch the miracle.

In the quiet
I feel your beauty,
your love in my life and my hand
a sweet caress
a kiss savored
my head in a grandmother's lap
someday
in warmth held.

In the quiet
life is more.

## Henry's backyard

Under a bright blue sky
we flew combat missions
never leaving the ground
for the planes
sat wingless
in Henry's backyard
safely cuddling
our imaginations
flying high
in the skies of war.

**What a world**

The Mickey Mouse Club
every night
my heart a flutter
Rin Tin Tin on Saturday mornings
and Sky King my favorite
eyes glued to the tube
and the puddle of water
on the garage floor
the shock of my life
a record player
my teacher
electricity nearly stopped my little heart
even worse than the goose
that chased me.

## Living in between

Between
what is true
what is false
a third path lies
discovered beyond our understanding
where truth eludes us.

# They Cry Out

## The Box

A star adorns its lid
safely keeps
stones and pebbles
my hearts
hopes and desires.

## Text it

Dressed in her best dancing dress
she scans the rows
hats over eyes
snores on their lips
the possibilities slim to none
texting her only hope
at least her fingers get to dance.

## Home

Freedom found in the wilderness
became more sweet after
a stop at Manzanar
a bitter cold wind
an ominous sky
my transition
home safe
to never forget.

## A title written in haste

A title written in haste
what a line
a poem must be lurking
so I beat the bushes of my mind
only to find
it is still a great line
nothing more.

## That moment

Three I found
would have been just enough
the fourth brought rain
dampening my mood
I wished I was home.

## Providence

It has been right there
in front of me for years
never realized
unknown
kept for me to discover
in my own sweet time
no regrets
providence.

## Out the car

Like a shot
she escaped
the door flung open
left
our car
in the middle of the road
wounded
like a bird with broken wing
and me
tweeting
mommy
come back
from the back seat.

**Never easy**

Thinking the correct order is the goal
I mistook a turtle
for a stone
in the brook
splash.

Feeling driven
along the path
I scurried
believing the destination was what mattered
the darkness overtook me
mindlessly my path
it turned out
was not a plan at all.

Doing
what I was told
what I was good at
focusing on success
being perfect
avoiding trouble
brought me more doubt
feeling inadequate in my labors
finally lead me to true healing
for me doing what came naturally
was illusion
the easy way.

## Musing Sara Teasdale

Having learned
what to be
and done my best
settled in the world
I returned
to rest once again
before
commingling
perhaps this time
forming a wandering soul
together will embark
a new journey
to learn and
find peace
a grain of sand
on a tawny spit
a chip traveling there
on the beach
seeking calm
amidst the breaking waves.

## It's Greek to me

As the Greeks
bemoaned Life
only to suffer too long
the cold hard ground
this the worth of life.

My relations believed
life an adventure
to be lived
both in time
and out
beyond
in and through
blending
a plot to make worthy
nothing wasted.

## Pollywog Pond

Off to catch pollywogs
me in my "don't get dirty" clothes
once there
knee deep in mud
a in can full of holes
hunting our prey
my buddy
and partner in crime says pointing,
"isn't that your daddy's car?"
and there it was
where no car had ever gone before
from behind the Mattel Toy Factory
in a cloud of dust
my daddy's Studebaker rides toward us
High Ho Silver...Away
I went
home in tears
no Happy Trails for me.

## The Bucket

A story about a bucket
hanging on a nail
down in a meadow
for over a hundred years.

Once a boiling pot making
field hand's eggs
a meal made in the field
eaten in the cool
under a tree at noon.

Now the maker
converts dead bugs
the leavings of birds
twigs and mice droppings
seeds grass and hair
cooking
the collected ingredients
into new life
soil
in the unyielding torture
of a long hot August day.

## Motorhome mommas

Same shape and height
different clad
composing a sixties revival
a session in the woods
the threesome performed
swaying to the sounds
high on the blues and beer
sharing tales of concerts
and conquests past
sex drugs and rock 'n roll
their separate stories combined.

Wishing
the three agreed
sadly
they should have married Jim Morrison
remembering his motorhome
was the best equipped.

## Obligation

Obligation completed
now branded traitor
for leaving my comfortable post
a big change
choice becomes.

## Taken

Pain comes
a reminder of all the steps
taken for granted
until now.

Endless steps
now appreciated
taken during long sleepless nights
my daughter in my arms
taken up switchback trails
thinking only of the pack on my back
taken down shady lanes
a whistle on my lips
nature filling my eyes
taken round the dance floor
my love in my arms
believing it will never end.

Now regret visits me daily
in the guise of pain
reminding me
a wish for more to take
I go down each path
noticing value in each one
taking in each step precious
noticing each and every one
taken.

## Aged

A girl wrapped in Kevlar
Gender the chink in her armor
Endless sense of betrayal
Duty destroyed.

## Remember

From tight lips
Silence comes kicking to my ears
Reminding me of what I missed
Out of sync
Regret
I thank God.

## Henry's mouth

It was his eyes that did it.

The bad word his mouth uttered
long forgotten
my mom called his
off to the bathroom he went
his little hand in hers
accepting his fate
his mouth open
empty
the bar of soap
his punishment
the mouth now full
spitting and coughing
but it was his eyes
that said it all.

## Gated

Who would have thought
the gates at Pendleton
and the entry to any country club
serve the same purposes.

## Minding

I have done it for years
mindless of the hurt I cause
now my mind sees
a fish being
just as I am
a human being
we become a part of the One
and this changes it all.

To eat is one thing
hunger acceptable
for sport
entirely different.

Noticing
taking joy in catching
but a sight of my relations
they in the wet
I in the dry of earth
sharing it all
both of us on our way
home.

## Hidden

Rewriting what is there
hoping to discover something more
something better.

## Fearing something bad will happen

Fear makes
protecting good sense
creates conflict so
a nightlight in the darkness
makes your room safer
until our father's idea lights
save electricity
so click the switch
his nimble fingers find
and your first and worst
nightmare
crashes in
something bad happens
out of the good.

## Fourteen

Years march
trampling me
told it is for the best
be underfoot
like earth
accept my role
trodden.

## Standing

Head crowned with purple hair
mouth filled with juice
her tribe surrounds her
she all ablaze
becoming heir
to Dinah's glory
she too
is going out.

## Missing period

We missed the point
noticing
the period ended it
only to allow something new
that little point
so strong
ended our chances
period.

## Outpost

At the point of no return
the last outpost
hope appears disguised
wishful thinking
births hope.

## Paper napkin

Scrawled in haste
the names of my childhood
now lost
hiding somewhere
or worse
in the trash
ironic
a few days ago
they were lost in my mind
memories forgotten
becoming urgent
just because they are now written
on a lost paper napkin.

## Vacant lot

Mostly a blank stare
reveals my disbelief
a lot
vacant
empty.

## No stone unturned

To make every possible effort
they say
while a gusher
hides in the Gulf
every drop
an atrocity remains
under every rock
unturned.

## Our best possible self

Hiding in plain sight
ready to be found.

Regrets mistaken
as errors
become sign-posts
pointing the direction
toward better choices
happier outcomes.

**They go**

When children our feelings are felt
not understood
unknown they go
unnamed
invisible.

# *After Thoughts*

## A Maker of time

The making of time
earth wind fire
water the key
unlocked
creation becomes
a matter of time.

## It is 3 o'clock

It is unavoidable
time's the messenger
or the enemy
choose one
and move on.

## Installer

Out my window
what a sight
his cap on tight
against the wind
trying not to spill
the man went tumbling
and the dish ran away with the ladder.

## Gravity

Apparently misjudging
the gravity of the situation
her therapist suggested
she feel the safety of the chair
hoping to ground her
empower her
build self-esteem
instead she floated
hopelessly
adrift in emotional nothingness
defenseless against the memories
now as before
a little girl
abused
and alone.

## Searching

Searching
the concrete jungle
bare
so secure.

The tiger in the bush
whispers
words echo in my gut
no good deed
goes unpunished.

## Key at the corner of 24<sup>th</sup> Street

Darkness hides it from me
and me from it.
its teeth all a glow
gnashing to rip open my leg
there in the street
just before
24<sup>th</sup> Street
the entrance
to my route.

The key
don't get caught
fast soundless
quick to get to the other side
safety on 24<sup>th</sup> street
that's the lock
the mean dog
out to bite me.

I could go way round
be chicken
deliver my paper route
that way round
let the dog win
only
I would know.

My choice to ride
swift and straight
the best use of the key
a key of bravery
to outwit
and outride the dog
overcoming my fear
unlocking a future
filled with challenges
met.

## Hard to do

Seeing the One in everything
so hard to do
especially when it is human
having empathy
becomes
the most important thing
for doing
everything.

## Whispering

Sitting
so quiet
I could hear the whispering
from the worn wooden wheels
of the motionless old table
behind him
just out view
softly
reminding me
both his mom and mine
once were young
children playing
laughing cut loud
with joy
fearlessly
they held nothing back.

## Random thoughts

Breaking away
rolling
brake free into life
ready and willing.

Grieving is
so long.

Spiders on crack
knitting needles going wild
webbing a mess
what fun!

Long shadows
drawing to a close
an even longer day
filled with worry
pain and loss.

## My view

Whipped by the wind
rain drops free
dance across the sky
some captured sadly
by my window screen
like in a net
trapped there with the dust
blown in on yesterdays
all now held
the pane an unwilling canvas
becomes mired
soot darkens my view
none have choice.

## The quest

In pursuit
my childhood invites me
reach back
relive them
own them
instead of living now
wishing for certainty
while all the time
questioning my own memories
filling up my time
avoiding the unknown.

From stillness
comes a whisper
do you want or do you seek?
safety or adventure?
desperate for both
turns quest to merry go round
round I go
forward leads to back
reaching for the rings
new and bright
they turn tarnished
brass symbols of yesterdays
remembered and known
not really living
though.

Breaking out
on the quest
amidst the roar of paper tigers
feeling the freedom of joy
together
necessary
they beckon me
have it and absorb it
transforming each
brass ring into a shining chain
be fasted and fastener at once
connected to it all
in that moment
so becoming.